CONTENTS

SESSION 1
WHAT'S FAITH

NOTES

initial thoughts

WHAT'S FAITH

GETTING STARTED

Throughout our mentoring study, we will spend a great deal of time exploring the Bible and consistently referring to it; therefore, it is imperative that we spend some time discussing a very important truth about the Bible.

We will also address the concept of faith throughout this study. Hebrews 11:1 defines faith as "the assurance of things hoped for, the conviction of things not seen." Although we may not be able to comprehend all the circumstances in our lives, we can feel certain that our Lord constantly has our well-being in mind.

MEMORY VERSE: Write and memorize Romans 10:17.

_____

_____

_____

_____

For the purpose of this study, we will define faith this way.

FAITH DEFINITION:
Faith is choosing to live as though God's Word is true regardless of circumstances; regardless of emotions and regardless of cultural trends.

Hebrews 11:6
"And without _faith_ it is impossible to please him (God)..."

Romans 14:23
"...whatever does not proceed from _faith_ is sin."

2 Corinthians 5:7
"for we walk by _faith_, not by sight."

1

CORE CONCEPT:
The definition of faith is one that we will use repeatedly throughout the mentoring process, and it can be translated to every area of life.

Look up the following verses in the ESV translation of the Bible and fill in the blanks.

Psalm 18:30 *"This God—his way is _____"*

Psalm 19:7 *"The law of the Lord is _____"*

Psalm 119:160 *"The sum of your word is _____, and every one of your righteous rules endures _____."*

CONSIDER

When you sit down to work a jigsaw puzzle, if you try to figure out what the final picture is going to be by looking at each individual piece, you'll never be able to figure it out, even if you look at each and every piece. The pieces are so small and make no sense individually. Yet, once you put those small pieces together, you will know what the picture is supposed to be. When you work a puzzle, you have faith that the pieces, though individually nonsensical, work together to make a great picture.

Similarly, when the Christian learns to live by faith, he or she learns to trust that, even though each day, each circumstance, and each trial may not make sense individually, God has a great, amazing picture in mind. Learning to live by faith is learning to **choose to believe** that the Bible is true. When you learn to live by faith, you learn to choose what God says in His Word over all else.

For example, look up Jeremiah 31:3, and answer the question: "Does God love you?"

As you work to assemble a puzzle, the whole process is much easier if you look at the picture on the box. *In life, the*

Bible is like the box. God has a plan and a design for your life. If you keep your eyes on the box, you will have a precise pattern to follow. *Keep your eyes on the Bible!*

The annual Christian Bookseller's Convention showcases acres of newly released material. There are enough books released every year to fill an entire football field, row upon row. The great majority of those books are devoted to help the Christian live a Christ-like life; however, it is no secret that the lives of many who read these books do not look very different from those who have no relationship with Christ.

DISCUSS

Why, with all the help that is available to this generation, do you think people still struggle with living a successful Christian life? Write your answer below.

_____

_____

_____

_____

Many begin their Christian walk with great enthusiasm, yet often find that they are struggling to live by faith (which means to choose to live as though the Bible is true). By applying God's Word to our daily lives, we can walk by faith rather than be tossed about by our emotions, circumstances or the perception of those around us.

List some circumstances in your own life with which you are struggling. For example, perhaps you are having financial difficulties, trouble forgiving others or conflicts with your family members.

_____

_____

_____

Even though most of us recognize the role that faith plays at the moment of conversion, we seem to forget that faith is also essential to living the Christian life. Paul tells us in his letter to the Corinthians that "we walk by faith, not by sight" (2 Corinthians 5:7). God also makes this clear in Hebrews: "but my righteous one shall live by faith" (Hebrews 10:38). These passages clearly state that faith is critical to living the Christian life, but what does it mean to "walk by faith?"

We discover in Ephesians 2:8 that we enter the Christian life by grace through faith. This means that it is because of God's kindness that we become rightly related to Christ through faith. It is in believing in the promises of God that we become His children. "Therefore, as you received Christ Jesus the Lord, so walk in him" (Colossians 2:6).

Ask yourself: How did you begin your Christian life? How do you live your Christian life?

We walk with Jesus day-by-day, moment-by-moment, by grace through faith. Just as we accept Jesus Christ as our Savior by grace through faith, we also need to learn to live our lives as Christians by grace through faith. This will become clear as you discover the Faith Process in the following pages.

What follows is called the Faith Process. Romans 10:17 tells us: "So faith comes from hearing, and hearing through the word of Christ." Once we begin to renew our minds with what God says in the Bible, then we can learn to trust the Lord in every area of our lives with all our heart, rather than leaning on our own understanding. The Faith Process involves three simple, yet profound, steps that will radically transform the way you live your life. As you apply this process to different areas of your life, you will find that the promises of God are rich and liberating, that the life of faith is indeed a wonderful journey, and that our God, whom we serve, is a faithful Father.

DISCUSS

Robert is married and has four children. His relationships are strained because he has begun to focus on his family members' weaknesses. An atmosphere of bitterness and hostility has begun to grow in his home. Robert is in desperate need to apply God's Word to his situation and live by faith rather than by what he feels or only what he sees.

Can you relate to him? Does any aspect of his life seem similar to yours?

EXPLORE

THE FAITH PROCESS – STEP ONE: REVIEW THE DEFINITION
Faith, as defined by Easton's Bible Dictionary, is the "persuasion of the mind that a certain statement is true."[1] Genuine faith, though, never stops with the mind. **If faith is genuine, it always affects HOW the believer lives his or her life.** James writes that "So also faith by itself, if it does not have works, is dead" (James 2:17). In other words, faith is never merely an intellectual experience; it always changes one's life. The first step is to internalize what is meant by the word *faith*. Living by faith is meaningless unless the believer truly understands what *faith* means. A good way to begin the process of internalizing and understanding the life lived by *faith* is to memorize the definition of faith.

Write and memorize the definition of faith.

_____

_____

_____

_____

---

[1] Easton, M.G., M.A.D.D., Easton's Bible Dictionary, (Oak Harbor, WA: Logos Research Systems, Inc.) 1996

Faith is choosing to live as though God's Word is true regardless of circumstances, emotions or cultural trends.

What does it mean to live as though the Bible is true?

Regardless of the **circumstances** you may be facing, regardless of the **emotions** you may be feeling, and regardless of the **cultural trends** that may be influencing your life, you **choose** to live as though the Bible is true by **faith**.

THE FAITH PROCESS – STEP TWO: ASK THE FAITH QUESTION
The next step in the faith process will help you to turn to the Bible as the object of your faith and begin living as though it is true, regardless of your circumstances, your emotions, or the cultural trends that surround you. In order to live this way, you should begin asking the Faith Question in every situation in your life:

If I lived as though the Bible is true, what would that look like in my life?

In Romans 12:2, Paul tells the believers: 'Do not be conformed to this world, but be transformed by the renewal of your mind...'" Notice how Paul connects *how a person thinks* to *how a person lives*. In other words, Paul is exhorting us to reject living life according to the world and its standards. The way you reject living life by the world and its standards is by renewing your mind, or changing the way you think. Continually asking the "faith question" will help you to not only renew your mind, but it will also help you in your effort to reject conformity to this world and its trends. Read Romans 12:2 and answer the following questions.

DISCUSS

Should we let the world conform us to how it thinks?

_____

What does that mean?

_____

Should we renew our mind?

_____

What does it mean to renew our mind?

_____

Now ask yourself: *If I lived as though Romans 12:2 is true, what would that look like in my life?* Record your answer.

_____

_____

_____

_____

More specifically, think back to a time when you experienced a season of great stress. Look up Isaiah 26:3. If you had been living as though Isaiah 26:3 is true, how would you have lived during that time of great stress? Write your answer below.

_____

_____

_____

_____

THE FAITH PROCESS – STEP THREE: ASK FOR THE HOLY SPIRIT'S HELP
John's epistle contains one of Scripture's most wonderful promises. He writes, "And this is the confidence that we have toward him, that if we ask anything according to his will he hears us. And if we know that he hears us in

whatever we ask, we know that we have the requests that we have asked of him" (1 John 5:14–15). Since God is more concerned with our obedience than we are, we should have the confidence that He will hear us when we ask Him to help us live according to His Word, rather than by our circumstances, emotions or cultural trends. The third step is simply to ask the Holy Spirit of God to help you live as though the Bible is true. Just as Jesus reached out His hand and took hold of Peter when his faith was weak, He is ready and willing to do the same for you.

Let's consider the example of Peter when he walked on the water. Read Matthew 14:22–33, and answer the following questions:

What miracle had Jesus just completed?

_____

Why did Jesus send His disciples ahead of Him?

_____

How did Jesus approach His disciples?

_____

How did the disciples respond to Jesus?

_____

What did Jesus tell Peter to do?

_____

This story is a perfect illustration of what happens when we live by our circumstances and our own understanding instead of what God says in the Bible. After feeding 5,000 men, Jesus sent His disciples ahead of Him in a boat so He could pray. When He finished praying, He walked to His disciples on the water. As He approached, the disciples saw Him and were understandably afraid of what they were seeing. As Peter started walking on the water, he was a perfect example of living by faith. Jesus had given

Peter the command to come to Him, and even though his circumstances seemed unusual and even difficult, he chose to believe Jesus' words were true by walking to Him.

After Peter began to walk on the water, he soon began to look at his circumstances, and he began to listen to his emotions and other pressures. To better understand what made Peter sink, identify the following:

What were the circumstances that Peter experienced?

_____

What were the emotions that Peter experienced?

_____

What were the cultural pressures that Peter experienced?

_____

The text remains silent on how the other disciples (who were of Peter's culture) were responding to Peter's actions, but it is clear that they did not follow him. The other disciples, many fishermen, understood the danger and death the sea could bring. In a previous situation, similar to this one, the disciples feared that they might drown because of the strong winds and waves (Matthew 8:23–26). They may even have been telling him to get back in the boat. This peer pressure could represent Peter's cultural circumstance, which would be counter to what Jesus was saying to him. As long as Peter chose to walk by faith, he could walk on water. The very moment he began to let his circumstances (he saw the water), his emotions (he was afraid) and cultural pressures (the peer pressure of the other disciples) become more significant than what Jesus said to him, *he began to sink.*

Any time we take our eyes off Jesus Christ and put them on our circumstances, our faith will waver, and we will begin to sink. Notice Jesus' response to Peter in Matthew 14:31. He took Peter's hand and said, "O you of little faith, why did you doubt?" According to Jesus, why did Peter begin to sink in the water?

Remember that faith is choosing to live as though the Bible is true regardless of circumstances, emotions or cultural trends. Jesus said that Peter began to sink because he had "little faith." Peter did not begin to sink because the wind was blowing or because of what the disciples might have been saying.

Based on the verses in Matthew 14:29-31, fill in the following blanks:

Jesus told Peter to _____

Peter began to let his circumstances consume him, and he began to _____ .

Consider the following chart that illustrates the difference between the reality of Peter's circumstance and what Jesus said to him:

Peter's Circumstance	What Jesus Said in Matthew 14:27–29
Wind was blowing. Asked to do the impossible. Fear was overwhelming. Discouragement was huge.	Take heart. Do not be afraid. Come.

We are asked to live out the impossible every day. The only way this can be done is by faith.

Peter's circumstance was that he was asked to do the impossible. Peter's fear and discouragement were overwhelming. Despite what Peter was experiencing, Jesus told him to take courage and not to be afraid. Then Jesus told Peter to come to Him.

In this lesson, as we have discussed the faith definition; we have laid a necessary foundation for the other biblical principles that we will discuss in the coming lessons. Throughout this study, you will discover how your relationship with God affects your relationship with others. Then, you will be able to apply these principles in your own life as you learn to make the decision to choose faith in every situation and circumstance of your life. Instead of acting on what your emotions, circumstances or cultural influences tell you, you are going to learn to trust God and to act on the truth of His Word.

YOUR LIFE TODAY
The Faith Process and the Certainty of Heaven

Let us look at some examples of how to work out this process in the reality of life. There may have been times in your life when you were fearful of what would happen to you when you died. What should you do when you feel fearful about your own death? First, you should recall the faith definition: **Faith is choosing to live as though God's Word is true regardless of circumstances, emotions or cultural trends.**

Secondly, you should ask the faith question: **If I lived as though 1 John 5:11–13 is true, what would that look like in my life?**

_____

_____

Lastly, **you should ask God to help you live as though this is true and to take hold of you, as He did with Peter,** when the circumstances of your life are causing you to sink. For example, you could pray something like this: *"Father, since you have promised me in 1 John 5:11–13 that I can live forever with You in heaven, I am choosing to live as though that is true. Would You help me make the choice to rest in the assurance of Your Word? Please remind me several times a day that I have a promised place in heaven because of Your Word."*

BEFORE YOU FINISH

The Faith Process starts now. Living by faith is a life-changing process; it is a process of taking the Bible and choosing of your own volition to live as though it is true regardless of circumstances, emotions or cultural trends. Faith is vitally dependent upon the Bible; therefore, you should make spending time studying God's Word a priority in your life, if it is not already. Start memorizing verses of Scripture that will help you in the Faith Process. Most importantly, begin the process today by asking God to show you areas where you are not already living as though the Bible is true. **Start the Faith Process now. Do it for the rest of your life.**

Review

Faith is choosing to live as though God's Word is true regardless of circumstances, emotions or cultural trends.

Ask

If I choose to live as though Romans 10:17 is true, how would I be living? How would these truths affect my life?

Pray

Take a moment to ask God to make these biblical truths a greater reality in your attitudes and actions. Share your thoughts below.

Consider all the material through which you have just worked, and read the following statement. When you completely agree with the statement, sign on the line.

Today, I am making a new commitment to choose to live as though the Bible is true regardless of my circumstances, my emotions and the cultural trends in my life. I know that I can do this by the power of God's Holy Spirit.

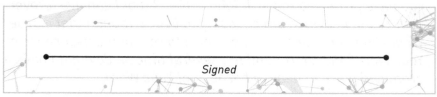

Signed

NOTES

Prayer Notes

SESSION 2

CAN YOU TRUST
THE BIBLE?

NOTES

initial thoughts

CAN YOU TRUST THE BIBLE?

This session will help you develop a better understanding of the divine origin and authority of the Bible. As you gain a better understanding of the purposes of the Word of God, you will develop a greater appreciation for the Bible and how you can use it in your own life.

Memory Verse: Write and memorize 2 Timothy 3:16–17.

_____

_____

_____

_____

FAITH DEFINITION:
Faith is choosing to live as though God's Word is true regardless of circumstances; regardless of emotions and regardless of cultural trends.

Hebrews 11:6
"And without *faith* it is impossible to please him (God)..."

Romans 14:23
"...whatever does not proceed from *faith* is sin."

2 Corinthians 5:7
"for we walk by *faith*, not by sight."

Core Concept:
God has given us the Bible so that we may know who He is and be equipped to do what He says because of who He is.

Refer to Session 1, "The Key That Unlocks the Door to a Successful Life" and answer the following question in the space provided.

TWO

If I lived as though 2 Timothy 3:16–17 is true, what would that look like in my life?

_____

_____

_____

_____

2 CONSIDER

Frank got up early every morning to read his Bible. His wife, Erica, was confused about why he would lose sleep just to read a book. She, too, had tried to read the Bible at different times throughout her life, but its references to the "Holy Spirit" and "the Lamb of God" made it seem so mysterious and mystical. Even though she liked some of the stories in the Old Testament, she felt it was always better to talk to a real live person rather than try to search the Bible's pages for answers when she really needed guidance and help. Sure it had some good stories and morals, but she believed that it must have been altered and modified throughout the years. Now that Frank seemed to enjoy his morning reading sessions, and he seemed joyful and content, she felt even more confused. I never felt that way about my Bible. What's wrong with me? She began to wonder.

Frank, on the other hand, could not understand why Erica was having such a problem with the fact that he wanted to read God's Word. Frank was growing tired of Erica's skepticism. Plus, he was frustrated that she did not seem to appreciate how much his daily Bible reading was helping their relationship. Frank wondered: Can she not see that I am more patient and content than ever? Why is it so hard for my wife to see that I am learning how to be a better person through my daily time reading the Bible?

How does Frank feel about Erica's confusion concerning his Bible reading?

_____

_____

How would Erica feel about Frank's frustration toward her?

_____

_____

Before going further in this lesson, it is important that you read the article "Can We Trust the Bible?" located at the end of this chapter.

DISCUSS
What new information did you learn from reading the article "Can We Trust the Bible?"

_____

_____

What information was the most surprising to you about the article?

_____

_____

EXPLORE
Is the Bible Reliable and Accurate?
Year after year, people have attempted to cast doubt upon the legitimacy and credibility of the Bible. People have wondered how they can know that the Bible is the same as when it was originally written, and they do not know if they can trust a book that seems to be full of myths. These concerns are addressed in the supplemental article "Can We Trust the Bible?" Use the facts of this article to answer the following questions.

DISCUSS

What questions or concerns did you have concerning the reliability of the Bible prior to reading the article?

_____

_____

_____

_____

Which aspects of the uniqueness of the Bible did you find most helpful?

_____

_____

Refer back to the previous story about Frank and Erica. Now what would you say to Frank and Erica?

_____

_____

Is the Bible the Word of God?

_____

Jesus and the authors of the Scriptures clearly claim that the Bible is the inspired Word of God. These claims by themselves do not establish the divine inspiration of the Scriptures. However, since the Bible clearly claims divine inspiration, it must either be inspired or be in error. Consider the following:

1. Is the Bible God-Inspired?

2 Timothy 3:16 states that all Scripture is inspired by God (NASB), and inspired, when translated from the original language means God-breathed. This gives us the mental picture of God breathing His life into the writings of the authors. Just as the wind fills the sails of a sailboat and

propels it, so the Spirit of God filled and moved the authors to write what they did. The writers, however, did not merely take dictation. Naturally, the words in the Bible reflect the temperaments, education and cultures of the people who wrote them, but the result is exactly what God intended.

Take the time to fill in the following charts based on 2 Timothy 3:16. If necessary, refer back to the similar chart in the first lesson. Note the perception of your experience in the left box, and the truth of God's Word in the right box:

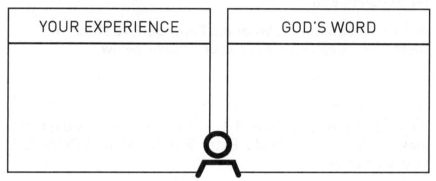

YOUR EXPERIENCE	GOD'S WORD

2. Do the Old Testament authors claim their writings are the Word of God?

Old Testament writers used many phrases to indicate that they believed they were writing God's words. For example, hundreds of times, Old Testament writers used the phrase, "Thus says the Lord..."

Read the following verses and fill in the spaces with words or phrases that indicate that the authors believed they were writing the words of God:

Deuteronomy 4:1

_____

_____

_____

2 Samuel 23:1-2

_____

_____

_____

3. Does the New Testament claim the same divine authority as the Old Testament?

New Testament writers also claimed that they were writing the words of God.

Read 2 Peter 1:16-21. What did Peter believe about Old Testament prophecy? Write your answer below.

_____

_____

If I lived as though 2 Peter 1:16-21 is true, what would that look like in my life? Read 2 Peter 3:16. What does Peter call Paul's writings?

_____

_____

_____

_____

If I lived as though 2 Peter 3:16 is true, what would that look like in my life?

_____

_____

4. Did Jesus acknowledge the reliability and divine authority of the Old Testament Scriptures?

Jesus made extensive use of the Scriptures. Read Matthew 5:18. What did Jesus say in this verse to indicate that the Bible is reliable? Write your answer below.

_____

Read Matthew 22:23–32. What did Jesus say in verse 31 to indicate that the Bible is God's Word? Write your answer below.

_____

_____

_____

_____

Note on Matthew 22:23–32: The Sadducees were a Jewish religious group. They often asked Jesus questions with the intention of tricking Him. Jesus put an end to their hypocritical inquiries by quoting from the Old Testament book of Exodus. During the time of Jesus, the book of Exodus was already several hundred years old. Jesus boldly said that Exodus was not just God's revelation to those who were alive in the days of Moses, but also to those who were alive then.

5. Is the Bible true?

The Bible attests numerous times to its correctness, trustworthiness and flawlessness. For examples of these claims, read the following verses in an ESV Bible and fill in the blanks:

Psalm 18:30 – The Word of the LORD is _____

Psalm 19:7 – The Word of God is _____

Psalm119:160 – The Word of God is _____ and _____

Given all these facts, you must still come to the place where you have to make a faith decision to accept the Bible as true or untrue, divine or fake, powerful or insignificant. You must choose of your own free will to have the faith to believe that the Bible is God's divine Word to you.

6. What Role Does the Bible Play in My Life?

Why did God give us His Word? The Bible plays a variety of roles in our lives. The following list is not comprehensive but addresses some important topics. Read the following verses and fill in each blank with the appropriate word.

God's Word reveals _____ to us.
—John 5:39

God's Word _____ us for every good work. —2 Timothy 3:16–17

God's Word is a _____ for our feet and a _____ for our path. —Psalm 119:105

If I lived as though John 5:39, 2 Timothy 3:16–17 and Psalm 119:105 are true, what would that look like in my life?

YOUR LIFE TODAY

Review 2 Timothy 3:16–17. Notice that the Bible is useful for our teaching, reproofing, correcting and training. These four equipping roles are illustrated in the following diagram:

1. TEACHING
shows you the path

4. TRAINING IN RIGHTEOUSNESS
staying on the path

3. CORRECTING
how to get back on the path

2. REPROOF
where you've gotten off the path

What Place Should God's Word Have in My Life?

Prioritize God's Word

Read Deuteronomy 32:44–47. What did Moses call God's Word?

_____

If I lived as though Deuteronomy 32:44–47 is true, what would that look like in my life?

_____

_____

Read Psalm 119:9–11. Where did David say he kept God's Word? Why?

_____

_____

If I lived as though Psalm 119:9–11 is true, what would that look like in my life?

_____

_____

DISCUSS

What does it mean that God's Word is in your life?

_____

_____

What things in your life are most important to you?

_____

_____

How might God's Word play a more important role in your life?

_____

_____

Obey God's Word

Read the following passages and fill in the chart:

	Luke 6:46–49	Psalm 1:1–6
What are the results of obeying God's Word?		
What are the consequences of not obeying God's Word?		

Obeying God's Word helps you build a strong spiritual foundation (Luke 6:46–49) and produce spiritual fruit even in times of trial (Psalm 1:1–6). If you do not obey God's Word, your spiritual foundation will be weak and unsteady (Luke 6:46–49) and you will not be able to produce lasting spiritual fruit (Psalm 1:1–6).

Read God's Word

It is impossible to develop a friendship with someone whom you never talk to; in the same way, it is impossible to grow in your relationship with God if you do not spend time reading the Word of God.

BEFORE YOU FINISH

Consider the following points to help you begin the practice of regular and consistent Bible study:

1. Read the Bible every day, even if it is only for a few moments.

2. Minimize distractions by choosing a time and place where there will be the fewest interruptions.

3. Before you start, pray for understanding.

4. The life and ministry of Jesus is a great place to start, so consider reading the Gospels (Matthew, Mark, Luke and John) first.

5. As you read, reflect on the following questions:

   » What does this passage tell me about God's love for me?

- » What life lessons are taught?
- » What is my response to this passage?
- » How do I apply this passage to my life?

6. Keep a journal.

7. Spend part of your time praying to God about:
   - » What you have just read
   - » Your concerns
   - » Your needs and the needs of your friends and family
   - » The salvation of your friends and family

My Action Plan for Regular Bible Reading
If you are not already doing so, choose a time of day to read.

What time of day will you read your Bible?

_____

If you do not have a good location, choose a good location to read. Where will you read the Bible?

_____

If you have not already begun to read a specific book, choose a book of the Bible to read. What book of the Bible will you read?

_____

Be Accountable for Your Bible Reading Plan
Be sure to discuss your Bible reading time with your discipleship partner at your next meeting.

What did you read?

_____

_____

How did God speak to you?

_____

_____

How did you apply your reading to your life?

_____

_____

Consider all the material through which you have just worked, and read the following statement. When you completely agree with the statement, sign on the line.

By faith I choose to believe that the Bible is God's inspired Word. I believe that it is given to me to help me live a life that is honorable to Him.

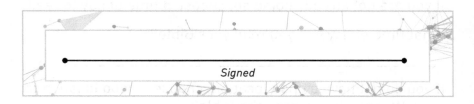

Signed

CAN WE TRUST THE BIBLE?

It has been called "The Greatest Book Ever Written." Kings and rulers have sought to destroy it with intense fervor. Men, women, and children have been put to death for affirming its teachings. Scholars have devoted their lives to proving or disproving its contents. It claims to be the Word of God and the source of absolute truth. If this book has made such astonishing claims about itself, one must ask, "Is it reliable? Where did it come from? Did the events described in the Bible really take place? Can I trust that it is God's Word?"

In order to answer these questions, the Bible needs to be examined in terms of its uniqueness, preparation, and confirmation through history, archeology, and prophecy. These avenues of exploration will demonstrate the reliability of the Bible and why it has earned the respect and allegiance of millions throughout history.

UNIQUENESS OF THE BIBLE

The study of the reliability of the Bible begins with its uniqueness. Webster defines unique as "different from all others; having no like or equal." The Bible is different from all other human writings in its continuity, circulation and survival.

A. ITS CONTINUITY

The first area of uniqueness of the Bible is its continuity. It is an amazingly unified document, despite factors which would lead to great disharmony in ordinary writings. Josh McDowell, noted author and lecturer on the historical evidences of the Christian faith, outlines some of these factors. He explains that the Bible was:

1. Written over a 1,600-year span;
2. Written by more than 40 writers from every walk of life—from king to peasant; philosopher to fisherman;

3. Written in different places—from the wilderness, to a comfortable room, to a dungeon;
4. Written at different times—from war to peace;
5. Written during authors' different moods—from the height of joy to the depths of despair;
6. Written on three continents—Asia, Africa, and Europe;
7. Written in three languages—Hebrew, Aramaic, and Greek;
8. Written concerning hundreds of controversial issues.[1]

Although the Bible contains this much diversity, its authors speak with harmony and focus on one theme: "God's redemption of man."[2] F.F. Bruce, Professor of Biblical Criticism at the University of Manchester, summarizes the Bible's continuity:

"The writings themselves belong to a great variety of literary types. They include history, law, religious poetry, didactic treatises, lyric poetry, parable and allegory, biography, personal correspondence, personal memoirs and diaries. ... For all that, the Bible is not simply an anthology; there is a unity which binds the whole together. An anthology is compiled by an anthologist, but no anthologist compiled the Bible."[3]

B. ITS CIRCULATION
The second area of uniqueness for the Bible is its circulation. It has been read by more people and published in more languages than any other work.[4] At the end of 1993, United Bible Societies reported that 2,062 languages had access to at least one book of the Bible. The Cambridge History of the Bible reports, "No other book has known anything approaching this constant circulation."[5] Although the widespread circulation of the Bible does not prove it is the Word of God, it does substantiate further the uniqueness of the Bible.

C. ITS SURVIVAL
The survival of the Bible is the third way it is unique from all other books. Composed before the invention of the printing press, it was written on perishable material such

as papyrus and parchment. For hundreds of years, it was copied and recopied by hand. Yet, this did not diminish its soundness. It has more manuscript evidence than any other piece of classical literature. John Warwick Montgomery, former Chairman of Church History at Trinity Evangelical Divinity School, makes this statement:

"To be skeptical of the resultant text of the New Testament is to allow all of classical antiquity to slip into obscurity, for no documents of the ancient period are as well attested bibliographically as the New Testament."[6]

The accuracy of the Old Testament manuscripts is the result of the Jewish system of preservation. Bernard Ramm explains this system:

"Jews preserved it as no other manuscript has ever been preserved. With their massora [methods of counting] they kept tabs on every letter, syllable, word and paragraph. They had special classes of men within their culture whose sole duty was to preserve and transmit these documents with practically perfect fidelity. ... Whoever counted the letters and syllables and words of Plato or Aristotle? Cicero or Seneca?"[7]

Not only has the Bible weathered the elements, but it also has withstood constant scrutiny and persecution. John W. Lea, author of *The Greatest Book in the World*, cited H.L. Hastings's explanation:

"Infidels for eighteen hundred years have been refuting and overthrowing this book, and yet it stands today as solid as a rock. Its circulation increases, and it is more loved and cherished and read today than ever before ... So the hammers of the infidels have been pecking away at this book for ages, but the hammers are worn out, and the anvil still endures. If the book had not been the book of God, men would have destroyed it long ago. Emperors and popes, kings and priests, princes and rulers have all tried their hand at it; they die, and the book still lives."[8]

TRANSLATIONS OF THE BIBLE

Not only does the uniqueness of the Bible support its reliability, but the methods of translation of this book also support its dependability. As previously outlined, the Bible was written over centuries by a variety of people. The original writings were composed in Hebrew (most of the Old Testament), Aramaic (parts of Ezra, Daniel and Jeremiah), and Greek (the whole New Testament).[9]

These writings have since been translated into most of the world's known languages. This causes some to question the accuracy of the Bible. They ask, "If the Bible has been translated so many times, version upon version, how can one possibly trust its reliability?" The answer to this question is found in the translation process. While the Bible has been translated into numerous languages, these translations are only one, or at most two, steps removed from the original text.

The Bible was translated into other languages soon after it was written. The Old Testament was translated into Greek during the third century B.C. From 383-400 A.D., Jerome, the secretary to the bishop of Rome, translated the Bible into Latin.[10] In 1382, John Wycliffe translated the Bible from Latin into English so the people could study the Bible in their own tongue. The Renaissance brought a renewed interest in the classics and the desire to study them in their original languages.[11] William Tyndale, who studied Hebrew and Greek, translated the Bible into English directly from ancient Greek texts.[12] Other English translations followed in quick order, but probably the greatest of all English translations was commissioned by King James of England in 1604 and was first published in 1611.[13]

Each of these works was taken carefully from the oldest writings of the Old and New Testament. Since the study of Greek and Hebrew was revived in the 15th century, scholars have been able to work directly from ancient manuscripts. Therefore, the belief is unfounded that today's Bible is based on a series of previous translations. We can be confident the Bible translations we have today are accurate and based directly on ancient manuscripts.

A further question arises, "Why are there so many current translations and why do they seem to vary at times?" Wycliffe produced his work because of his desire to present a translation in the common tongue.

Current translations are made with a similar motivation to produce a fresh version in the language of today. A careful comparison of a translation from 1960 with a more current translation would show subtle differences in word choice. Comparing both to the much older King James Version would show even greater differences.

Today's translations also will vary somewhat based on whether the translators made a *word for word* (NASB, KJV, NKJV, ESV) translation or one based on a *thought for thought* (NIV, NLT, TM) concept. The meaning remains the same, but word choices will vary.

CONFIRMATION OF THE BIBLE THROUGH HISTORY

A. BIBLIOGRAPHICAL TEST
The third means for verifying the reliability of the Bible is its confirmation by historical test. Josh McDowell, a well-known Christian apologist and evangelist, argues that the Bible should be subjected to the same tests as any other historical document to determine its reliability. These tests are the bibliographical test, the internal evidence test, and the external evidence test.

1. **New Testament bibliographical test.** McDowell describes the bibliographical test as "... an examination of the textual transmission by which documents reach us."[14] This is accomplished by examining the number of manuscripts and the time interval between the original and the existing copy. The manuscript evidence

of the New Testament is astounding. Today there are more than 5,000 manuscript copies of portions of the New Testament in Greek and at least 15,000 more in other languages. No other ancient writing has anywhere near this abundance of existing manuscript evidence. Additionally, the interval of time between the composition of the New Testament books and the date of the earliest existing manuscripts is the shortest of any work of antiquity. Sir Frederic G. Kenyon, who was the Director of the British Museum, summarizes the manuscript evidence as follows:

"The interval then between the dates of original composition and the earliest extant [existing] evidence becomes so small as to be in fact negligible, and the last foundation for any doubt that the Scriptures have come down to us substantially as they were written has now been removed. Both the authenticity and the general integrity of the books of the New Testament may be regarded as finally established."[15]

2. **Old Testament bibliographical test.** This test for the Old Testament is more complicated. Given the age difference between the New and Old Testaments, the number of surviving manuscripts for the Old Testament is much smaller.

Despite the small number of manuscripts (as compared to the New Testament), the accuracy of the Old Testament documents has been verified through the discovery of the Dead Sea Scrolls in 1947. The Scrolls consist of approximately 40,000 inscribed fragments. More than 500 books have been reconstructed from these pieces. The Dead Sea Scrolls provide confirming evidence that Old Testament manuscripts date before the time of Christ.

Gleason Archer, Chairman of Old Testament at Trinity Evangelical Divinity School, reports that the Isaiah copies "... proved to be word for word identical with our standard Hebrew Bible in more than 95 percent of the text. The 5 percent of variation consisted chiefly of obvious slips of the pen and variations in spelling."[16] Dr. Henry Morris, President of the Institute for Creation Research, concludes, "There is thus no reasonable doubt that our present Old Testament ... is practically identical with the text in use several centuries before Christ, practically extending back to the time when the last books of the Old Testament were originally written."[17]

B. INTERNAL EVIDENCE TEST

The second test for the historical accuracy of the Bible is the internal evidence test. This test determines whether the written record is credible by analyzing the ability of the writer or the witness to tell the truth. The New Testament relies upon men who were eyewitnesses of the actual events and teachings of Jesus, or men who related eyewitness accounts of these details. Throughout the New Testament, the writers refer to what they had seen and heard. Many of their contemporaries also had witnessed Jesus' life. If they reported the facts incorrectly, these people would have challenged their writings. F.F. Bruce explains, "The disciples could not afford to risk inaccuracies (not to speak of willful manipulation of the facts), which would at once be exposed by those who would be only too glad to do so."[18]

An additional indication of the sincerity of the New Testament writers is their willingness to record incidents that portray themselves in a negative light, such as their flight after Jesus' arrest, their competition for a high place in the Kingdom of God, and Peter's denial of Christ.[19] Given these facts, we can trust the New Testament writers' portrayal of Christ.

C. EXTERNAL EVIDENCE TEST

The external evidence test is the final one that historians use to verify the reliability of a document. This test seeks other historical material to substantiate the information contained in the document under review. One example of such confirmation is the testimony of a friend of the apostle John (who wrote five books in the New Testament). Irenaeus, who was the Bishop of Lyons in A.D. 180, was a disciple of John and wrote the following:

"Matthew published his gospel among the Hebrews ... in their own tongue, when Peter and Paul were preaching the gospel in Rome and founding the church there. After their departure ... Mark, the disciple and interpreter of Peter, himself handed down to us in writing the substance of Peter's preaching. Luke, the follower of Paul, set down in a book the gospel preached by his teacher. Then John ... himself produced his gospel, while he was living at Ephesus in Asia."[20]

Along with the testimony of contemporaries, archeology also provides powerful external evidence for the reliability of the Bible. (This confirmation will be discussed at length in the following section.) Archeologist Joseph Free reports, "Archeology has confirmed countless passages which have been rejected by critics as unhistorical or contradictory to known facts."[21] Finally, the weight of historical evidence clearly upholds the reliability of the Bible as Dr. Clark Pinnock states:

"There exists no document from the ancient world witnessed by so excelling a set of textual and historical testimonies and offering so superb an array of historical data on which an intelligent decision may be made. An honest [person] cannot dismiss a source of this kind. Skepticism regarding the historical credentials of Christianity is based upon an irrational (i.e., antisupernatural) bias."[22]

THE WITNESS OF ARCHEOLOGY TO THE BIBLE

Archeology provides the fourth avenue of exploration of the reliability of the Bible. Archeology not only verifies certain biblical references, but it also provides a background for the message of the Bible.

A. THE OLD TESTAMENT RECORD

William F. Albright, one of the world's greatest Near East archeologists, states, "There can be no doubt that archeology has confirmed the substantial historicity of Old Testament tradition."[23]

With more than 25,000 sites already discovered that show connections to the Old Testament period, the amount of archeological support is overwhelming. To demonstrate how archeology has confirmed the Bible, the controversy surrounding Abraham can be cited. Critics of the 19th century felt that Abraham could not have existed as he is described in the Bible. For example, they felt he would be unable to read and would lack knowledge of law and history.

Sir Leonard Woolley's excavations at Ur of the Chaldees show that it was a highly developed city. They discovered clay tablets that served as books and receipts for business transactions. Therefore, "it became clear that Abraham was a product of a highly developed culture. ..."[24] Sir Frederic Kenyon concurs:

"It is therefore legitimate to say that, in respect of that part of the Old Testament against which the disintegrating criticism of the last half of the nineteenth century was chiefly directed, the evidence of archeology has been to re-establish its authority..."[25]

Another example of the contribution of archeology is the discovery of the Ebla tablets in 1974. For years, the Genesis 14 account of the victory of Abraham over Chedorlaomer and the Mesopotamian kings has been held to be fictitious and the cities of Sodom, Gomorrah, Admah, Zeboiim, and Zoar as mere legend.[26] However, the Ebla tablets refer to all five of these cities and in one document even lists them in the same sequence as Genesis 14.[27]

Lastly, in August 1993, it was reported that an Israeli archeologist had discovered the first known reference outside the Bible to King David. The inscriptions were found on a broken monument in northern Israel. Hershel Shanks, editor of *Biblical Archaeology Review*, said, "The stele [monument] brings to life the biblical text in a very dramatic way. It also gives us more confidence in the historical reality of the biblical text."[28]

B. THE NEW TESTAMENT RECORD

The New Testament has also been substantiated by the archeologist's spade. The Acts of the Apostles most readily lends itself to archeological investigation because it contains so many references to customs, places and events of that time. Therefore, Luke, the author of Acts, has been subjected to intense scrutiny. For example, in his gospel, it was believed that he was wrong about the events surrounding Jesus' birth. Critics maintained that there was no census at that time; people did not have to return to their ancestral home; and Quirinius was not governor of Syria.[29]

Archeological discoveries have upheld Luke's account on all three fronts. First, the evidence shows that the Romans held a census every 14 years and that the practice was initiated under Augustus. Second, an inscription in Antioch names Quirinius as governor of Syria in 7 B.C. and 6 A.D. Finally, a papyrus found in Egypt reads this way:

"Because of the approaching census it is necessary that all those residents for any cause away from their homes should at once prepare to return to their governments in order that they may complete the family registration of the enrollment."[30]

Sir William Ramsay, who has completed the most extensive study, thus far, of the data recorded in Acts, concedes, "Luke is a historian of the first rank ... In short, this author should be placed along with the very greatest of historians."[31]

Other references in the New Testament to certain cities and regions, customs and political situations have also been confirmed through archeology. In fact, Morris says, "... no statement in the New Testament has to this date been refuted by an unquestioned find of science or history. This in itself is a unique testimony to the amazing accuracy and authenticity of the New Testament records."[32]

CONFIRMATION OF THE BIBLE THROUGH PROPHECY

The final area of confirmation of the reliability of the Bible is prophecy. The inclusion of many specific prophecies sets the Bible apart from all other works. The fulfillment of these prophecies points to the reliability of the other information presented in the Old and New Testaments. The number of prophecies is astounding. Therefore, the following analysis is limited to a few messianic prophecies and prophecies related to a specific city. The fulfillment of these prophecies will amply demonstrate the reliability of the Word of God.

A. PROPHECIES CONCERNING THE MESSIAH

The Old Testament contains more than 300 prophecies of the coming Messiah that were fulfilled in Jesus. For purposes of this discussion, a few of these prophecies have been selected. Their fulfillment is explained in the New Testament excerpts that are included.

It should be remembered that the prophecies were written by a variety of men over several centuries. At least 400 years passed between the last of these prophecies and the appearance of Jesus.[33]

PROPHECY	FULFILLMENT
#1 BORN OF A VIRGIN "Therefore the Lord himself will give you a sign. Behold, the virgin shall conceive and bear a son, and shall call his name Immanuel." —Isaiah 7:14	"... she was found to be with child from the Holy Spirit...Joseph...knew her not until she had given birth to a son. And he called his name Jesus." —Matthew 1:18, 24, 25
#2 BORN AT BETHLEHEM "But you, O Bethlehem Ephrathah, who are too little to be among the clans of Judah, from you shall come forth for me one who is to be ruler in Israel, whose coming forth is from of old, from ancient days." —Micah 5:2	"....Jesus was born in Bethlehem of Judea ..." —Matthew 2:1
#3 HANDS AND FEET PIERCED "... they have pierced my hands and feet." —Psalm 22:16	"And when they came to the place that is called The Skull, there they crucified Him ... " —Luke 23:33
#4 GARMENTS PARTED AND LOTS CAST "they divide my garments among them, and for my clothing they cast lots." —Psalm 22:18	"When the soldiers had crucified Jesus, they took his garments and divided them into four parts, one part for each soldier; also his tunic. But the tunic was seamless, woven in one piece from top to bottom, so they said to one another, "Let us not tear it, but cast lots for it to see whose it shall be ..." —John 19:23, 24
#5 BONE NOT BROKEN "He keeps all his bones; not one of them is broken." —Psalm 34:20	"But when they came to Jesus and saw that he was already dead, they did not break his legs." —John 19:33 (Historical note: The executioners normally broke the criminals' legs to hasten their death.)

(All Scripture quotations in this chart are from the English Standard Version.)

Given the fulfillment in Jesus' life of these and many other prophecies, it becomes evident that God directed what has been written by the prophets. Josh McDowell makes this conclusion:

"Certainly God was writing an address in history that only the Messiah could fulfill. Approximately forty major claims to be the Jewish Messiah have been made by men. Only one—Jesus Christ—appealed to fulfilled prophecy to substantiate His claims, and only His credentials back up those claims."[34]

B. PROPHECIES CONCERNING THE CITY OF TYRE

In addition to the messianic prophecies, the Bible also contains many prophecies regarding the fate of certain cities and nations. As an example of the astounding accuracy of these biblical prophecies, the following is an analysis of the predictions related to the city of Tyre. This city of ancient Phoenicia is now in southern Lebanon. It was once an enemy of Israel.

In Ezekiel 26 (KJV), written between 592 and 570 B.C., the Lord declares His anger toward Tyre for her extreme arrogance. He predicts her invasion by Nebuchadnezzar, the king of Babylon, and her ultimate destruction. Verses 7, 8, and 14, declare her fate:

"For thus says the Lord God, 'Behold, I will bring upon Tyre from the north Nebuchadnezzar king of Babylon... and he will make siege walls against you ...'

'And I will make you a bare rock; you will be a place for the spreading of nets. You will be built no more, for I, the Lord, have spoken,' declares the Lord God."

The fulfillment of Ezekiel's prophecy is explained by the *Encyclopedia Britannica*. It states, "After a 13-year siege (585-573 B.C.) by Nebuchadnezzar II, Tyre made terms and acknowledged Babylonian suzerainty [sovereignty]." It goes on to say:

"In his war on the Persians, Alexander III ... marched southward toward Egypt, calling upon the Phoenician cities to open their gates ... The citizens of Tyre refused to do so, and Alexander laid siege to the city. Possessing no fleet, he demolished old Tyre, on the mainland..."[35]

Philip Myers, a secular historian, summarizes the fate of Tyre:

"Alexander the Great ... reduced [Tyre] to ruins. She recovered in a measure from this blow, but never regained the place she had previously held in the world. The larger part of the site of the once great city is now bare as the top of a rock—a place where the fishermen that still frequent the spot spread their nets to dry."[36]

The record of history regarding Tyre makes it obvious that each prophetic detail recorded in Ezekiel was fulfilled just as the Bible predicted.

CONCLUSION

The Bible's uniqueness, its preparation, and the testimony of history, archeology and prophecy, all work together to confirm beyond reasonable doubt that it is totally reliable. Sir Frederic G. Kenyon makes this conclusion:

"... it is reassuring at the end to find that the general result of all these discoveries and all this study is to strengthen the proof of the authenticity of the Scripture, and our conviction that we have in our hands, in substantial integrity, the veritable Word of God."[37]

* The preceding article is taken from the *Practical Christian Living* curriculum. Used with permission from Mentoring One 2 One.

END NOTES:

1. Josh McDowell, Evidence That Demands a Verdict, 1972, p. 16.
2. Bill Wilson, ed., The Best of Josh McDowell: A Ready Defense, 1990, p. 28.
3. Wilson, op, cit., p. 28.
4. McDowell, Evidence, p. 18.
5. McDowell, op. cit., p. 19.
6. Wilson, op. cit., p. 30.
7. Ibid.
8. Ibid., p. 3-31.
9. Charles C. Ryrie, Concise Guide to the Bible, 1983, p. 17.
10. Ryrie, op. cit., p. 21.
11. Norman L. Geisler and William E. Nix, From God to Us: How We Got Our Bible, 1974, p. 230.
12. Geisler and Nix, op. cit., p. 231-232.
13. Ryrie, p. 21-22.
14. Josh McDowell, More Evidence That Demands A Verdict, 1975, p. 47.
15. Wilson, p. 44.
16. McDowell, Evidence, p. 58.
17. Henry Morris, Many Infallible Proofs: Evidences for the Christian Faith, 1974, p. 41.
18. McDowell, More Evidence, p. 52-53.
19. Ibid., p. 54.
20. Wilson, p. 54.
21. Ibid.
22. Ibid., p. 55.
23. Ibid., p. 92.
24. Paul Little, Know Why You Believe, 1968, p. 52.
25. Wilson, p. 93.
26. Ibid., p.98.
27. Ibid.
28. John N. Wilford, "Israeli Archeologist Finds First Evidence Outside Bible for King David's Dynasty," New York Times News Service: Austin American-Statesman, August 8, 1993, p. A17
29. Wilson, p. 109
30. Ibid.
31. Morris, p.26.
32. Ibid., p. 26-27
33. Wilson, p. 210-211.
34. Ibid., p.211.
35. Ibid., p.61
36. Ibid.
37. Morris, p.23.

NOTES

Prayer Notes

SESSION 3

CAN YOU BE SECURE IN YOUR RELATIONSHIP WITH CHRIST?

NOTES

initial thoughts

CAN YOU BE SECURE IN YOUR RELATIONSHIP WITH CHRIST?

In this session, we will explore the claims Jesus made about Himself, and we will learn the key principles of being eternally secure in our relationship with God. We will find out how we can have confidence that our relationship with God is secure and unchangeable regardless of our emotions, experience or performance as His followers.

GETTING STARTED

Memory Verse: Write and memorize 1 John 5:11–13.

_____

_____

_____

_____

FAITH DEFINITION:

Faith is choosing to live as though God's Word is true regardless of circumstances; regardless of emotions and regardless of cultural trends.

Hebrews 11:6
"And without _faith_ it is impossible to please him (God)..."

Romans 14:23
"...whatever does not proceed from _faith_ is sin."

2 Corinthians 5:7
"for we walk by _faith_, not by sight."

CORE CONCEPT:

Entering into an eternal relationship with God is a gift, which we receive at the moment we trust Jesus to pay the penalty for our sins. **This gift will last forever.**

CONSIDER

Steve attended church with his parents when he was a child, but he quit going to church when he graduated from high school. It was a relief for him to get away from home and begin to make his own decisions. When he was 25, he landed his dream job, and a year later, he married his high school sweetheart. Life could not have been better.

A few months into his marriage, however, things began to fall apart. Steve and his wife had heated arguments on a regular basis. The pressures from his job began to mount as he was asked to take more responsibility, and this resulted in additional time away from home. Eventually, the word *divorce* started to come up in the arguments with his wife. This was not how he had envisioned his marriage.

When all this was happening, a friend from work invited him to hear a Christian speaker. At this meeting, Steve made the decision to become a follower of Jesus. Initially, he was excited to explore his relationship with God. He attended a weekly Bible study with his friend, and he started to see some positive changes in his personal life, work and marriage.

Over time, however, the arguments with his wife escalated again. As frustration on the job returned, he began going out after work rather than home to his wife. During this time, Steve attended the funeral of his grandfather. Although a solemn occasion, many people celebrated his life as a man who desired to follow God. As friends and family recounted memories of his grandfather, they also expressed their assurance that he was in heaven.

Steve began to question if he had a relationship with God in the same way that he had a relationship with his grandfather because he was not confident that his life had changed since his decision to follow Jesus. After all, his actions did not seem to match how he thought a Christian should live. He started to wonder if Jesus were really in his life, and at times, he questioned whether he had ever had a relationship with God in the first place.

DISCUSS
How would you counsel Steve?

EXPLORE
Is Security Possible?
Like Steve, many Christians have questions as to the certainty of their relationship with God. Some may ask, "How can Jesus be in my life when my performance is so dismal?" Others wonder, *How can forgiveness and eternal life be a gift? There has got to be more to it than accepting Christ.* Many fear being cut off from God's love when they die.

It is not uncommon for followers of Jesus to struggle with these thoughts. When these thoughts come, how should Christians respond? To answer this question, it is helpful to look at the role of your mind and your emotions in your relationship with God.

The Role of Your Mind
Christianity is not a blind leap of faith. It is a personal relationship with the God of the universe, revealed in space and time through Jesus Christ. It would be foolish to believe or trust in someone or something if there were no rational basis for that belief. For example, a person may believe with all his heart that he can jump off a tall building and not get hurt. Unfortunately for him, the law of gravity, not his leap of faith, will dictate the outcome of his decision to jump. We first need to ask if there is any rational basis for following Jesus. Let us look at the claims Jesus made about Himself and see what evidence He provided to support those claims.

Read the following Scriptures and note what claims Jesus made about Himself.

John 10:30–33

_____

_____

_____

_____

John 14:6-9

_____

_____

_____

_____

John 11:23-26

_____

_____

_____

_____

Mohammed claimed to be a prophet; Buddha was an agnostic; Confucius was an ethical teacher. Jesus claimed to be God. Since Jesus was the only one to confidently claim His divinity, He is the only one who risked His reputation. If Jesus lied about being God, then He placed everything He stood for in jeopardy. If He claimed to be God, and then was proven to be wrong, His whole ministry would have been destroyed.

Read the following verses and note what evidence the following passages provide to support Jesus' claims:

Matthew 8:23-27

_____

_____

_____

_____

Luke 5:17-26

_____

_____

_____

1 Corinthians 15:3–6

_____

_____

_____

_____

Think back to the time when you accepted Christ into your life. What do John 5:24 and 1 John 5:11–13 say Jesus did for you the moment you accepted Him as your Savior?

_____

What is the significance of knowing you have eternal life rather than just hoping or wishing that you have eternal life?

_____

The Role of Your Emotions
Emotions can be defined as feelings or reactions to events or experiences.

Since God created emotions, they are a very important part of your life and your experiences. Because emotions change often, however, they are not a valid basis for determining whether or not you have a relationship with God.

The following illustration shows the relationship between fact (God and His Word), faith (our trust in God and His Word) and feeling (the responses to our experiences).

Use 1 John 5:13 to illustrate this relationship:

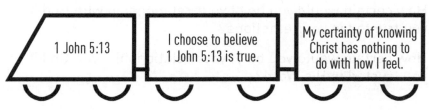

Do not depend upon feelings. The promise of God's Word, not our feelings, is our authority. The Christian lives by faith (trust) in the trustworthiness of God Himself and His Word. This train diagram illustrates the relationship between **fact** (God and His Word), **faith** (our trust in God and His Word), and **feeling**. The train will run with or without the caboose. However, it would be futile to attempt to pull the train with the caboose. In the same way, we, as Christians, do not depend upon feelings or emotions, but we place our faith (trust) in the trustworthiness of God (fact) and the promises of His Word.

"Probably no one thing has caused more people to lack the assurance of a vital, personal relationship with God through Jesus Christ than a wrong emphasis on emotions. Seeking an emotional experience contradicts faith—the very thing that pleases God. The Bible says, "And without faith it is impossible to please God..." (Hebrews 11:6).

—Bill Bright

You can be sure of your relationship with God if you have responded to His offer of forgiveness through Jesus. The promise of God's Word, not your feelings, is your authority.

Finish the following statement: I know that I will go to heaven because

_____

_____

_____

_____

DISCUSS

How certain would you be of your relationship with God if you trusted in your emotions?

How certain would you be of your relationship with God if you trusted in His Word?

In a world full of uncertainty and hopelessness, to be able to live a life in which you are certain of your eternal salvation is revolutionary. Those who are able to grasp and hold to the assurance of their salvation are those who are able to live a life of hope and purpose.

Write Ephesians 2:8–9 on the following lines:

_____

_____

_____

_____

_____

_____

What happens if we do not accept God's gift of forgiveness?

_____

Consider the following illustration:

In 1830, George Wilson was tried by the U.S. court in Philadelphia for robbery and murder and was sentenced to hang. Andrew Jackson, the president of the United States, granted him a presidential pardon. Wilson refused it, insisting that it was not a pardon unless he accepted it. The question was brought before the U.S. Supreme Court, and Chief Justice John Marshall wrote the following decision: "A pardon is a paper, the value of which depends upon its acceptance by the person implicated. It's hardly to be supposed that one under sentence of death would refuse to accept a pardon, but if it is refused, it is no pardon. George Wilson must hang." What was the outcome? George Wilson was hanged.

Your Security with God
From the moment you receive Jesus by faith you can rest in the certainty that you will spend eternity with God.

REVIEW

Faith is choosing to live as though the Bible is true regardless of circumstances, emotions or cultural trends.

Write John 6:37–40 on the following lines.

_____

_____

_____

_____

_____

_____

If I lived as though John 6:37–40 is true, what would that look like in my life? Record your thoughts below.

_____

_____

_____

_____

_____

Write John 10:27–30 on the following lines.

_____

_____

_____

_____

_____

_____

If I lived as though John 10:27–30 is true, what would that look like in my life? Record your thoughts below.

_____

_____

_____

_____

_____

Write Romans 8:38–39 on the following lines.

_____

_____

_____

_____

_____

_____

If I lived as though Romans 8:38–39 is true, what would that look like in my life? Record your thoughts below.

_____

_____

_____

_____

_____

Write 1 John 5:11–13 on the following lines.

_____

_____

_____

_____

_____

If I lived as though 1 John 5:11-13 is true, what would that look like in my life? Record your thoughts below.

_____

_____

_____

_____

Applying the Faith Definition to Your Security with God

As you reflect on what John 6:37–40, John 10:27–30, Romans 8:38–39 and 1 John 5:11–13 say about your security with God, fill in the following chart. Note the perception of your experience in the left box, and the truth of God's Word in the right box:

YOUR EXPERIENCE	GOD'S WORD

YOUR LIFE TODAY

Which word best describes how certain you are that Christ is in your life?

_____ positive

_____ hopeful

_____ confused

_____ doubtful

If you died right now, how certain are you that you would spend eternity with God?

_____ positive

_____ hopeful

_____ confused

_____ doubtful

If you have never made the decision to receive God's gift of forgiveness through Jesus, or if you are unsure of it, continue reading to learn more.

Receiving Jesus involves turning from yourself to God and trusting Jesus to come into your life, forgive your sins and make you who He wants you to be. Just to agree intellectually that Jesus is the Son of God and that He died on the Cross for your sins is not enough. Nor is it enough to have an emotional experience. You receive Jesus by faith.

You can receive Jesus right now, or you can make certain that you have a relationship with Jesus, by faith, through prayer. Prayer is simply talking with God. God knows your heart and is not as concerned with your words as He is with the attitude of your heart. The following is a suggested prayer:

Jesus, I want to know You personally. I admit that I have sinned against You and am separated from You. Thank You for dying on the Cross for my sins. I open the door of my life and receive You as my Savior and Lord. Thank You for giving me eternal life and making me part of Your family. Take control of my life. Make me the person You created me to be.

If you are not certain, take a moment to pray right now, and Jesus will come into your life as He promised.

If you just prayed to receive God's gift of forgiveness through Jesus, you have entered into a never-ending relationship with your Creator. You are now part of God's family. Hebrews 13:5 says that God "will never leave you nor forsake you". You can know that your relationship with God is secure and unchangeable regardless of your feelings, experiences or performance as His follower.

Now, pray this prayer, and sign and date on the appropriate lines:

"Father, I choose to believe that Jesus Christ died for me. I have placed my faith in Jesus and what He did on the Cross for me, and I believe I will go to heaven when I die. Thank You that I have the security that I know for certain I will go to heaven."

Signed _____

Date _____

BEFORE YOU FINISH

Consider all the material through which you have just worked, and read the following statement. When you completely agree with the statement, sign on the line.

By faith I choose to believe that I can be secure in my relationship with God. I know that God wants me to enjoy absolute confidence in my relationship with Him.

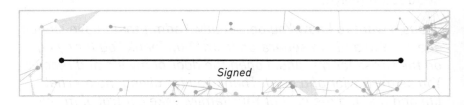
Signed

NOTES

Prayer Notes

SESSION 4

KNOWING WHO
YOU ARE IN CHRIST

NOTES

initial thoughts

KNOWING WHO YOU ARE IN CHRIST

In this session, you will discover more about your identity as a Christian and how you are to view yourself as a follower of Jesus. Because of the forgiveness that God has provided for you through His Son, you can live securely in the confidence that God eternally loves you. Therefore, you do not need to focus on your own faults and failures.

GETTING STARTED

Memory Verse: Write and memorize Galatians 2:20.

_____

_____

_____

_____

FAITH DEFINITION:
Faith is choosing to live as though God's Word is true regardless of circumstances; regardless of emotions and regardless of cultural trends.

Hebrews 11:6
"And without *faith* it is impossible to please him (God) ..."

Romans 14:23
"...whatever does not proceed from *faith* is sin."

2 Corinthians 5:7
"for we walk by *faith*, not by sight."

CORE CONCEPT

When you became a follower of Jesus, you gained a new identity in Jesus Christ.

CONSIDER

Jacob has always been an excellent baseball player. When he was 10 years old, his baseball team, the Blue Jays, made it into the league championship game. On the day of the game, Jacob showed up excited to play. "Coach, I'm here, and I'm ready to go!"

There was only one problem; Jacob was not wearing his uniform. He was wearing a new uniform that his grandfather had given him for his birthday. Instead of the regulation blue and white jersey and pants that the league had provided for him, he was decked out, head to toe, in red. Jacob had on a red cap, red shirt, red pants, red socks and red shoes.

"Jacob," his coach said, "your red uniform is very nice, but you cannot wear it in the game today. You have to wear the team uniform like everyone else." Jacob protested, "But, Coach, I like this uniform. My granddad gave it to me." "Jacob," the coach replied, "we are playing the Cardinals; if you will look across the field you will see the entire team is decked out in red!"

Jacob had a problem. He did not know who he was. He did not understand his identity.

Do Christians face a similar situation? Why or why not?

_____

Your identity is extremely important in your life to help you establish and define who you are. When you become a Christian, you take on the identity of Jesus Christ. You have all the privileges and responsibilities that come with such an identity. Many Christians, like Jacob, do not understand their identities, and they go through life not truly understanding who they really are. If you do not understand and embrace your identity in Jesus Christ, you will have trouble completing all that God has intended for you to experience and accomplish.

EXPLORE

When we become Christians, we gain new identities, and God adopts us as His own children. Since we carry His name, we should strive to reflect His character. Of course, there are times when we do not act or feel like children of God. Fortunately, no matter how we behave, once we gain our new identity in Jesus at salvation, we can never behave badly enough to lose that identity.

In Galatians 2:20, Paul wrote:

"I have been crucified with Christ. It is no longer I who live, but Christ who lives in me. And the life I now live in the flesh I live by faith in the Son of God, who loved me and gave himself for me."

Paul mentions some important truths in the Scripture. Let us explore these truths and their significance to our daily Christian lives.

YOU HAVE TAKEN ON A NEW IDENTITY

The New Testament Scriptures discuss our new identity in Jesus Christ. For the purposes of this study, we will look at a few of these identity truths.

1. You have been declared innocent of every charge against you.

Look back at Galatians 2:20. To be "crucified with Christ," means that when Christ died on the Cross, you died as well. Of course, you did not die in the flesh; you died to God's wrath and the power of sin over your life.

According to 1 Peter 2:24, what has Christ done with your sins?

_____

What is the result?

_____

Read the following verses and record what they say Christ has given to us.

2 Corinthians 5:21

_____

_____

_____

_____

Philippians 3:8–9

_____

_____

_____

If I lived as though 2 Corinthians 5:21 is true, what would that look like in my life?

_____

_____

_____

If I lived as though Philippians 3:8–9 is true, what would that look like in my life?

_____

_____

_____

The following image shows how God cannot look at us without seeing our sins.

Consider the following chart in regard to our state of sinfulness and righteousness:

The triangle represents the triune image of God.

The eye represents what God sees.

Sin represents your disobedience to God.

The person represents you.

Our sin separates us from God; therefore, when He looks at us, He sees our sin.

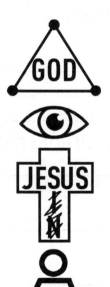

Then, when Jesus died on the Cross for our sins, He became the permanent sacrifice. We took on His righteousness. When God looks at us now, He sees us through the lens of the Cross.

Imagine that a jury has found you guilty of a crime that you committed. When the time comes for the judge to pronounce your sentence, you go to the courtroom to face him, but you are not alone; your defense attorney is with you. Suddenly, your attorney walks up to the judge and speaks to him. After they finish their conversation, the judge says to your attorney, "It is my understanding that you want me to put the penalty for what your client did on you, and you want to serve the sentence I am about to hand down. Is this correct?" Your defense attorney says, "Yes, I will pay the penalty." The guards then escort your attorney out of the courtroom so that he may pay your penalty. The judge looks at you and says, "You have been declared forgiven, and you are no longer responsible for paying the penalty of the crime you committed. In fact, you will walk out of this courtroom as if you never committed the crime."

Now, try to imagine that your attorney, who has paid for your mistake, is the judge's son.

Read 1 John 2:1–2. What is your attorney's name?

_____

Write 1 John 2:1–2 in the following blanks.

_____

_____

_____

_____

What role does Jesus play on our behalf to the Father?

_____

What is an advocate?

_____

What does that mean for us?

_____

DISCUSS

In your own words, clarify what it means that Jesus is holy.

_____

_____

_____

_____

Do you think of yourself as a holy person like Jesus?
Why or why not?

_____

_____

_____

_____

Read 2 Corinthians 5:21 and Philippians 3:8–9. The Bible
says that each Christian has been declared righteous and
enjoys a holy standing before God. Do you believe that for
yourself? Why or why not?

_____

_____

_____

_____

What would your life be like if you were to see yourself as
a person who is holy before God?

_____

_____

_____

_____

Write a thank-you paragraph to God that includes all that Christ has done for you based upon this lesson.

_____

_____

_____

_____

2. Sin no longer has power over you.
Read Romans 6:11–13.

DISCUSS

Based on Romans 6:11–13, explain the phrase that you are "dead to sin."

Many people would like to believe that being dead to sin means you no longer have a desire to sin. Unfortunately, this is not true. Since you have died to sin, and Christ lives His life through you, you no longer have to yield to sin when you are tempted. You now have the power to choose not to sin.

3. You have hope.
If you have invited Jesus into your life, you can **know** that you will spend eternity with Jesus. While you are free from the power and punishment of sin during this lifetime, you will also enjoy the absolute absence of sin in heaven.

Read the following Scriptures and record what they say about your eternal life.

Ephesians 2:12–13

_____

_____

_____

_____

1 Peter 1:3–5

_____

_____

_____

_____

DISCUSS
What does it to mean to have hope?

_____

What happens when a person is hopeless?

_____

YOUR LIFE TODAY
You Live Out Your New Identity by Faith in Christ

You have taken on the righteousness of Jesus as your new identity. Look at 2 Corinthians 5:21. If I lived as though 2 Corinthians 5:21 is true, what would that look like in my life?

"For in it the righteousness of God is revealed from faith for faith, as it is written, "The righteous shall live by faith." —Romans 1:17

God accepts us only on the basis of the death of Jesus Christ, His Son. It is a natural human response to believe that we should behave in certain ways in order to please Him and thus earn His acceptance and approval. If you believe that you must perform to earn God's acceptance and approval, then you will also believe that you must perform well enough to maintain His acceptance and approval.

DISCUSS

What are some things that people do in the pursuit of God's acceptance and approval?

_____

_____

Why is it that many Christians believe that if they do not perform adequately then they will not sustain God's approval?

_____

_____

Paul discussed the new Christian's position in Christ in Romans 6:1–18. Read this passage and keep in mind the following three principles that can help believers live in the reality of their new identities.

1. Reflect on the truths of your identity (Romans 6:3, 6, 8–9).

a. Your former sinful behavior does not have to have power over you because you have died with Christ.

b. You will never be alone again because you are joined with Christ in a new life forever.

c. You do not have to live your Christian life on your own strength because you have the power of Jesus available to live through you.

DISCUSS

Which of these truths are most encouraging to you?

_____

Which of these truths is the most difficult to believe about yourself?

_____

2. By faith, choose to see yourself in the light of your new identity (Romans 6:11).

Satan's goal is to convince you that you are unlovable, a failure and unacceptable to God. You may struggle with condemning thoughts concerning your past, or hopelessness concerning your future ability to deal with temptation. These thoughts are not based on the truth of God's Word. To combat this scheme of Satan, you must evaluate your thoughts, emotions and actions in light of the identity that God has given you through Jesus. When you find yourself slipping into the feelings and behaviors of your old identity, you have to renew your mind.

DISCUSS

Why is it sometimes easier to focus on the "old you" rather than the "new you"?

_____

_____

3. Yield to God's leadership (Romans 6:12–13).

A way to live out this principle is to offer up a daily prayer to the Lord before you begin your day. While it does not have to be exact, such a prayer could resemble the following:

Lord, thank You for the new identity You have given me because of Your Son. Thank You that when You look at me, You do not see my sin, but you do see Jesus. Help me to live as though that is true. I want to offer my life to You today. I give you my thoughts, my feelings, my attitudes and my actions. Please help me as I strive to yield to Your leadership today. Help me be an example of Your love to others. Amen.

Pray this prayer every day for the next month.

APPLYING THE FAITH DEFINITION TO YOUR IDENTITY IN CHRIST

Fill in the following chart based on what you have learned from Galatians 2:20–21. Note the perception of your experience in the left box, and the truth of God's Word in the right box:

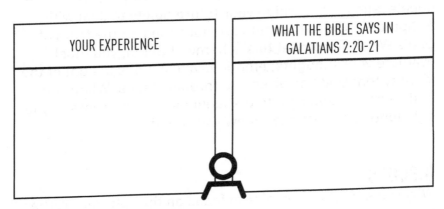

YOUR EXPERIENCE	WHAT THE BIBLE SAYS IN GALATIANS 2:20-21

BEFORE YOU FINISH

Consider all the material through which you have just worked, and read the following statement. When you completely agree with the statement, sign on the line.

By faith I choose to believe that, due to Jesus' death on the Cross, God looks at me through the lens of the Cross. When He sees me, He sees Jesus.

Signed

NOTES

Prayer Notes

SESSION 5
COMMUNICATING WITH GOD

NOTES

initial thoughts

COMMUNICATING WITH GOD

GETTING STARTED

The purpose of this session is to equip you to develop a more effective and intimate prayer life. While prayer is the way we communicate with God, it is not just the act of asking for what we want or need. Prayer is also listening to God so that we may develop a more intimate relationship with Him.

Memory Verse: Write and memorize Philippians 4:6–7.

_____

_____

_____

_____

FAITH DEFINITION:

Faith is choosing to live as though the Bible is true regardless of circumstances, regardless of emotions and regardless of cultural trends.

Hebrews 11:6
"And without *faith* it is impossible to please him (God) ..."

Romans 14:23
"...whatever does not proceed from *faith* is sin."

2 Corinthians 5:7
"for we walk by *faith*, not by sight."

Core Concept:
Prayer is a vital part of a Christian's relationship with God.

CONSIDER

Catherine was living the life she had always imagined she would. She worked mornings at a local radio station where she helped research stories for news broadcasts. In the afternoons, she stayed home and cared for her two young children. She was thankful for the opportunity to be able to work and spend time with her children. She and her husband had been married for eight years, and except for an occasional argument, they got along well.

Her spiritual life, however, was a different matter. She felt restless in her Christianity because she never felt connected to God. At church, people would talk about their relationship with God, but she did not feel like she had her own personal relationship with Him. During church, she enjoyed singing worship songs, but she still felt disconnected. She tried spending some time with God because she felt like it was something she needed to do, but she never knew what she should do once she opened her Bible.

"What does God want from me?" she thought. "Why does a relationship with God have to be so much work?" she asked herself.

One day, while driving home from work, Catherine heard a sermon on one of the local Christian radio stations about prayer. She learned that the reason she felt disconnected from God was that she spent very little time in prayer. Rather than taking the time to be still and quiet, her prayer life consisted of quick one-liners such as, "God, please get me out of this traffic," or "God, please help me get my kids to bed."

Catherine also learned that her time communicating with God was important to every area of her life. She began to set aside a few minutes every morning before work to read her Bible and talk to God about the day ahead. Soon, as her relationship with God became more intimate, she found herself getting up even earlier so that she could spend more time with Him.

Before too long, Catherine's restlessness was gone, and her relationships with her children and husband grew even stronger. She knew this was a discipline she needed to uphold, not just for a short time, but also as a priority going forward.

How would you assess your connection with God?

_____

_____

_____

Is God doing something to prompt a more intimate relationship with you?

_____

_____

_____

EXPLORE

1. WHAT IS PRAYER?

Prayer is simply having a conversation with God. When you enter into a relationship, the only way to keep it healthy and vibrant is to devote sufficient time and energy to it. When you became a Christian, you entered into a relationship with God. That relationship needs time, energy and communication, too.

It is still not uncommon for believers to struggle with their prayer life. The list of reasons why Christians struggle in their prayer life can include:

a. Some harbor unconfessed sin.

b. Some have difficulty verbalizing their thoughts, especially to someone they cannot see.

c. Some have been discouraged by previous failed attempts at communication with God.

d. Some do not believe that God cares enough about them to communicate with them.

"Prayer is communication with God."
— St. Clement of Alexandria

Whatever may be stalling our prayer lives, the Bible is clear that God wants to communicate with us through prayer. Let us take a closer look at the characteristics of a healthy prayer life.

Your communication with God is like a child to his or her father.

Psalm 103:13 states that "As a father shows compassion to his children, so the LORD shows compassion to those who fear him." Unfortunately, the term "father" sometimes leaves many people with the impression of someone who is harsh, disconnected or unavailable.

What impression do you get when you think of the word "father?"

Detached	Affectionate	Disdainful	Gentle
Accessible	Intolerant	Severe	Spiteful
Preoccupied	Accepting	Rigid	Sincere
Adoring	Barren	Concerned	Loving

Read the following passages and record the words used to describe God.

1 Peter 5:6–7

_____

_____

_____

_____

Matthew 7:7–11

_____

_____

_____

_____

Psalm 149:4

_____

_____

_____

_____

Consider the previous passages, and fill in the chart below.
Note your perception of your experience in the left box, and
the truth of God's Word in the right box:

YOUR EXPERIENCE	WHAT GOD'S WORD SAYS IN 1 PETER 5:6-7, MATTHEW 7:7-11, PSALM 149:4

If you were living as though 1 Peter 5:6–7, Matthew 7:7–11
and Psalm 149:4 were true, how would you be living?

_____

_____

_____

_____

You can talk to God about anything, at any time and in any place.

Read the following passage that Paul wrote in Philippians 4:6–7:

"do not be anxious about anything, but in everything by prayer and supplication with thanksgiving let your requests be made known to God. And the peace of God, which surpasses all understanding, will guard your hearts and your minds in Christ Jesus."

No matter what is going on in your life, God wants you to communicate with Him. You can talk to God about the good things as well as the bad things. You can go to Him when you have a pressing need, when you just feel like sharing a thought, or when you feel like you need to hear from Him.

Read the following verses and note any insights you may have concerning prayer.

Psalm 62:8

_____

_____

_____

Matthew 6:9–10

_____

_____

_____

Ephesians 3:14–19

_____

_____

_____

Colossians 1:9–12

_____

_____

_____

Hebrews 4:14–16

_____

_____

_____

James 1:5

_____

_____

_____

James 5:14–16

_____

_____

_____

2. WHY IS PRAYER IMPORTANT?

"More things are wrought by prayer than this world dreams of." —Alfred Lord Tennyson

Too many times, people think of prayer as a last resort. How many times have you heard someone say, "All I can do is pray?" Any energy you devote to prayer will accomplish more than anything else you might try to do to solve any of your problems because prayer is powerful. In addition to the power that prayer can bring to your life, there are other reasons why it is important. A few of those reasons are listed below:

Prayer glorifies God.

"Whatever you ask in my name, this I will do, that the Father may be glorified in the Son." —John 14:13

Prayer builds intimacy with God.

"Draw near to God, and he will draw near to you...." —James 4:8

God commands us to pray.

"pray without ceasing,"
—1 Thessalonians 5:17

"Continue steadfastly in prayer...."
—Colossians 4:2

Prayer enables us to have an impact on the world.

"... The prayer of a righteous person has great power as it is working."
—James 5:16

List any other reasons you believe prayer is important.

"To pray is to change. Prayer is the central avenue God uses to transform us. If we are unwilling to change, we will abandon prayer as a noticeable characteristic of our lives. The closer we come to the heartbeat of God, the more we desire to be conformed to Christ. To pray is to change." —Richard Foster

3. HOW ARE WE TO PRAY?

Since prayer is basically conversing with God, we have not been given a set of guidelines to follow, and there are no certain words or phrases that we have to say. It can be helpful, however, to follow a certain pattern in prayer to become familiar with the different aspects of communication. The acrostic ACTS is one such pattern. It stands for:

Adoration
Confession
Thanksgiving
Supplication

We will explore the ACTS acrostic in further detail.

Adoration

Adoration is simply praising God. It means honoring and praising our Father and offering Him recognition for all of His marvelous characteristics.

Read Psalm 145:1–9 and note the characteristics of God that cause you to want to praise Him.

_____

_____

_____

Give an example of a time when you were overwhelmed with the desire to praise God.

_____

_____

_____

Confession

The word "confess" means to agree with God about our sins. When you become aware of an action or an attitude that is displeasing to God, you need to confess it. We need to admit our sin to God because our sins are, ultimately, against Him. That way we can maintain sincere and candid conversations with Him.

King David expressed his heart's desire in Psalm 139:23–24:

"Search me, O God, and know my heart! Try me and know my thoughts! And see if there be any grievous way in me, and lead me in the way everlasting."

There are times when we will be aware of a sin immediately or soon after we commit it. However, it is also necessary to ask God to search through every crevice of our hearts. If we do so, He will be faithful to show us any sin we may have disregarded that needs to be confessed and repented of.

A prayer of confession does not have to be elaborate or wordy. Once God has revealed a sin, you merely have to talk to God about it. You might say, "God, I agree with You that when I did _____ I sinned against you."

Spend a few minutes right now, and ask God to search and cleanse your heart. If He brings anything to mind, confess it and accept His forgiveness and move on. Share any thoughts you have concerning any disregarded sin God revealed to you.

_____

_____

_____

_____

THANKSGIVING

Read the following Scriptures, and note what they say about expressing thanks to God.

Psalm 92:1

_____

_____

_____

1 Thessalonians 5:18

_____

_____

_____

DISCUSS

How can you be "thankful in all things?"

_____

_____

_____

What keeps you from feeling thankful?

_____

_____

_____

A prayer of thanksgiving will include the things in your life for which you are thankful. For example: "God, I thank You for the life You have given me. Thank You for Jesus, and all the changes He is making in my life. I also thank You for my family and friends who love me."

In the space below, write a prayer of thanksgiving.

_____

_____

_____

_____

_____

SUPPLICATION

Supplication is what happens when you make requests of God, and when you pray for your needs as well as the needs of others.

Read the following passages and note some of the requests we can make of God:

Matthew 6:11

_____

_____

_____

Matthew 6:13

_____

_____

_____

Colossians 4:3

_____

_____

_____

A prayer of supplication might look similar to the following: "God, please guide my pastor and church staff as they face the challenges of directing our church. Please guide our country's leaders to make the decisions that You want them to make. Please help me to overcome the guilt that Satan has been trying to place on me for not being a better Christian."

Write a prayer of supplication in the space below.

_____

_____

_____

_____

_____

_____

_____

4. WHAT HINDERS OUR PRAYER LIFE?

Satan does not want us to communicate with God, so he will attempt to throw many obstacles in our paths to hinder our prayer lives. Some of these things include the following:

- Doubt (James 1:6–8)

- Unconfessed sin (Psalm 66:18)

- Relational problems (1 Peter 3:7)

- An unhealthy fear of God (Hebrews 4:14–16)

- Past struggles (2 Corinthians 5:17)

How have any of these hindrances affected your prayer life?

_____

_____

_____

DISCUSS

What does Hebrews 4:14–16 say a believer should do if he or she is afraid to approach God?

_____

_____

_____

What hindrances seem to affect your prayer life most?

_____

_____

_____

YOUR LIFE TODAY

Based on what you have learned in this lesson about prayer, what has God led you to do concerning your own prayer life?

_____

_____

_____

If you were living as though Philippians 4:6–7 were true, how would you be living?

_____

_____

_____

BEFORE YOU FINISH

Take a few minutes and discuss the following questions with your mentoring partner:

1. In what area of prayer do you need to grow?

   _____

   _____

2. Share a time when God answered a prayer that concerned you.

   _____

   _____

3. What are some steps you can take to help make prayer a greater priority in your life?

   _____

   _____

Consider all the material through which you have just worked, and read the following statement. When you completely agree with the statement, sign on the line.

By faith I choose to believe that I know I am certain that God wants to communicate with me. Because I am a child of God, I can have a powerful, effective prayer life.

Signed

NOTES

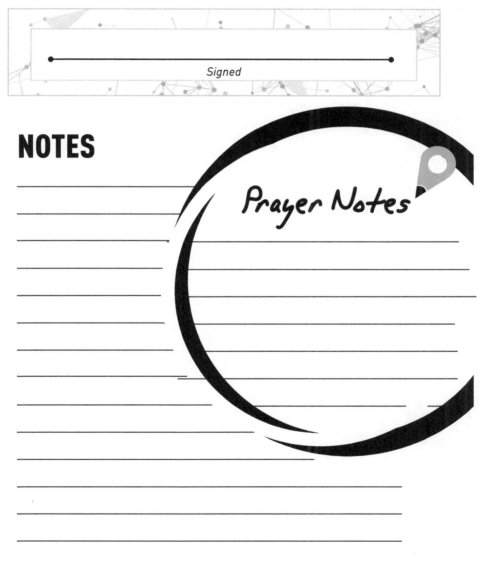

Prayer Notes

SESSION 6
MAKING DISCIPLES

NOTES

initial thoughts

MAKING DISCIPLES: MULTIPLYING YOURSELF SPIRITUALLY

GETTING STARTED

In this session, we will discover the concept of spiritual multiplication. Then, we will discuss the biblical pattern of spiritual multiplication that is found in 2 Timothy. Finally, we will explore the basis of our motivation to multiply spiritually.

Memory Verse: Write and memorize 2 Timothy 2:2.

_____

_____

_____

Faith Definition:

Faith is choosing to live as though God's Word is true regardless of circumstances; regardless of emotions and regardless of cultural trends.

Hebrews 11:6

"And without *faith* it is impossible to please him (God)..."

Romans 14:23

"...whatever does not proceed from *faith* is sin."

2 Corinthians 5:7

"for we walk by *faith*, not by sight."

CONSIDER

Donald sat in the pew and listened to the visiting preacher speak on Matthew 28:18–20. He had heard that this passage was part of what was called the Great Commission, but this preacher made it seem so urgent. He likened the Great Commission to a relay race in which members of a team must successfully pass the baton in order to complete the race. "The key to winning the race," he said, "is to pass the baton. If we do not pass the baton to the next generation of Christians, our society will be in trouble." Donald thought the Great Commission was for missionaries and preachers. It had never occurred to him that the Great Commission was meant for him. Now, he saw that he could leave a legacy and impact the next generation.

Read Matthew 28:18–20. In this passage, the main verb "make disciples" is a command. The verbs "go," "baptizing" and "teaching" are participles that tell you how to do the command.

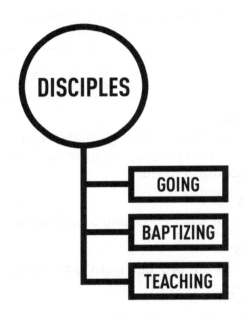

This passage means that we make disciples by:

Going

"Go" means being intentional about making disciples. We are to be intentional about making disciples as we go about our lives.

Baptizing

"Baptizing" addresses the principle of helping others to be introduced to and identified with Jesus Christ.

How does baptism identify us with Jesus?

_____

Why is it important for believers to be baptized?

_____

Teaching

"Teaching" means that we should teach other Christians to obey God's Word by faith.

Read 2 Timothy 2:2 and Acts 1:8. These verses are considered to be parallel passages to Matthew 28:18–20.

SPIRITUAL MULTIPLICATION DEFINED

Spiritual multiplication is mentoring that equips a believer to evangelize and mentor others so that they can evangelize and mentor others, and so on, and so on. _Spiritual multiplication is different from spiritual addition:_

Spiritual addition: Leading someone to faith in Jesus Christ or helping a believer spiritually.

Spiritual multiplication: Mentoring and preparing someone to mentor and prepare others who will, in turn, mentor and prepare others.

Anyone who wants to be involved in spiritual multiplication needs foresight as to how God wants to increase Himself through him or her. This involves fostering relationships, adhering to the truth, staying accountable, modeling godly living and having a desire to minister according to the pattern established in the New Testament.

Compare the following:

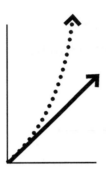

If you introduced 10 people each year to faith in Jesus for the next 10 years, you would see 100 people added to the church. VS. If you discipled one person per year for the next ten years, who were then equipped to reach and disciple one person per year, and so on, you would be part of raising up thousands of trained workers for the body of Christ in a 10-year period.

Which of the above represents spiritual multiplication?

EXPLORE

If you are going to understand what it means to spiritually multiply, you need to look at it from Paul's perspective in 2 Timothy 2:1–10. Read that passage, and note the necessary principles of spiritual multiplication.

1. Understand the Motivation of Grace.

"You then, my child, be strengthened by the grace that is in Christ Jesus." —2 Timothy 2:1

Someone who is passionate about mentoring does not mentor only because he has been commanded to do so; he does it because this is what he desires to do. He understands that God has done an amazing work in his own life, and he wants to share that with others.

Why do some Christians not share the Good News of God's grace with others?

_____

The image sequence below is a presentation of the *3 Circles: Life Conversation Guide from Life on Mission* The illustrations have been created to be a tool to share the Gospel with other people, and have been designed so that they can be simple enough to draw on the back of a napkin. An illustration of the 3 Circles presentation and a helpful app can be found at http://lifeonmissionbook.com/conversation-guide.

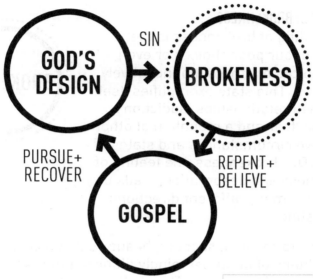

CIRCLE 1: GOD'S DESIGN

From the very beginning, God had a plan for humans. Not only did God have a plan for humanity at large, He had and *has* a plan for every human individually. God has a design for the way we should treat our families, work our jobs, and interact with friends and strangers; the plan is perfect. The Creator who knit together every being desires nothing more than for His plans to be implemented in every life.

Written by Dr. Jimmy Scroggins: copyright owned by NAMB, permission granted.

The challenge is that there is something within people that pushes us to depart from God's design, to go in our own direction. The Bible has labeled that departure from God's design "sin."

Sin leads to a world of consequences. When we sin, we find ourselves in a place of "brokenness."

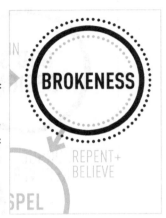

CIRCLE 2: BROKENNESS

The feeling of brokenness is the result of our poor choices or even the choices of others that negatively affect us. This state exemplifies itself in ruined relationships, addictions, unease, fear and a mountain of other negative circumstances and states of being. Our brokenness, the feeling of emptiness and desperation, leads us to look in many different directions for healing.

We turn to religion, success, beauty, substances, anger and a litany of other seemingly filling solutions to fix the brokenness in our lives. The challenge is that none of the solutions we carve out for ourselves will work; the brokenness remains.

Although brokenness is bleak, God uses it for good. God uses brokenness to help people understand that there is a problem that needs a solution. When someone surveys his life and recognizes the destruction around him and acknowledges that his solutions have failed, he often becomes open to the idea of a different path. He becomes open to a genuine change. The Bible's word for change is "repent."

We want to change and repent but we realize that we can't do much on our own (as evidenced by our own solutions to our brokenness). The good news is that God has a plan to fix the problem of brokenness; it's called the "Gospel."

CIRCLE 3: GOSPEL

The Gospel is the story of what Jesus did for us. Jesus, who is God in flesh, came and lived a perfect life. He never departed from God's design; He lived a life completely without sin. He taught people about God's love for them and His design for their lives. He healed the sick, spent time with the poor, and sought the outcasts. When He was around 33 years old, people that He loved nailed Him to a cross and murdered Him. While Jesus was on the cross, God did something incredible. He took the sins of the world and placed them on Jesus. So in His death, Jesus paid the penalty for all of our sin. After He had accomplished His mission on the Cross (bearing the consequences of the world's sins), Jesus died and was buried in a tomb. Three days later, Jesus rose from the dead. In His conquering of death, Jesus proved that He was who He said He was, the Son of God. Jesus proved that He could do what He said He could do, forgive sin. And this is the Good News.

The death and Resurrection of Jesus opens up the path by which we might return to the design of God. God's provision means that we can do no good of our own to fix brokenness, nor can we lose that provision by making mistakes. The path to restoration and redemption is this: Repent and believe.

When we make the step of turning from our sins (repentance) and turning toward Jesus (belief), God restores us. He does a work in our hearts that helps us to pursue and recover God's design. No matter what our brokenness looks like or how deep we are in it, God restores us to a right relationship with Him through Jesus.

When we come to faith in Jesus and are restored to His original design for us, we begin to experience the good things that God intends for us to have: purpose, forgiveness, community, hope, joy. As we experience these blessings from God, He sends us back into the brokenness of the world to help others discover the Good News that we have found.

STAGE	SUPPORTING VERSES
GOD'S DESIGN	Genesis 1:31; Psalm 19:1
SIN	Romans 3:23; Romans 6:23
BROKENNESS	Romans 1:25; Proverbs 14:12
GOSPEL	John 3:16; Colossians 2:14
REPENT & BELIEVE	Mark 1:15; Ephesians 2:8–9; Romans 10:9
RECOVER & PURSUE	Philippians 2:13; Ephesians 2:10

Many people understand what their culture expects of them (what they should or should not do), and they try to live by those expectations. They give money, volunteer or go to church because they feel they are expected to do so. Even though God wants us to do these things, He wants us to do them out of the overflow of our hearts. Once people are discipled, and they understand grace, they are free to give money, volunteer and go to church because they are grateful to God. They are also excited about all He has done for them, and they are overwhelmed with gratitude. For a greater understanding of this gratitude, go back and review the 3 Circles illustration.

Practice presenting the 3 Circles below:

2. Commit to a Life of Multiplication.

"and what you have heard from me in the presence of many witnesses entrust to faithful men who will be able to teach others also." —2 Timothy 2:2

Ben went to the wedding of a young man he had mentored two years earlier. Although he was happy to attend Jackson's wedding, he was sure he and his wife would not know anyone else at the wedding. During the reception, five of Jackson's friends introduced themselves to Ben and told him that they were all in different stages of the mentoring process. Jackson had discipled one of them; he discipled another, and so on, and so on.

If you want to multiply spiritually, you must commit your life to investing in the lives of others and encouraging them to do the same.

The chart below illustrates Paul's ministry of spiritual multiplication. Paul only needed to mentor Timothy. Then Timothy needed to develop disciples who would develop disciples. This chart also illustrates why the selection of those to be discipled is so critical. If someone decides not to share what they have learned with others by developing their own mentoring relationships, spiritual multiplication will stall.

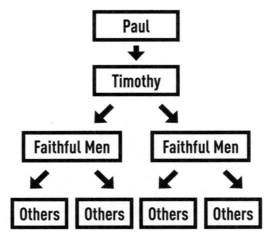

Prayerfully consider whom you would like to disciple. As you do so, think about the influence you could have many spiritual generations into the future. Begin now to pray for the person you will mentor and for the people he or she will mentor, and so on.

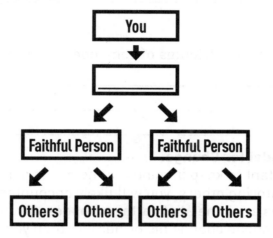

3. Look for the Potential in Others.

As you prayerfully begin to consider whom you will disciple, there are certain characteristics you should look for. There are three main characteristics to look for in the life of a person who is ready to be discipled. These characteristics are:

· Availability

· Teachability

· Faithfulness

List some of the attributes of someone who is available.

_____

_____

_____

Someone who is available will desire to be discipled. He knows he needs to mature spiritually and is excited to start the process.

List some of the attributes of someone who is teachable.

_____

_____

_____

List some of the attributes of someone who is faithful.

_____

_____

_____

4. Be a Model for Change.
It is important to keep in mind that no one is perfect. As you begin mentoring others, you will likely encounter people whose lives are in need of certain changes. If you want to help someone change his or her life, then you have to be committed to be a model for change. In order to show someone how to allow God to change them, you must allow God to change you.

Describe a time when someone else was used by God to help you change.

_____

_____

_____

5. Commit to Live a Disciplined Life.
"Share in suffering as a good soldier of Christ Jesus. No soldier gets entangled in civilian pursuits, since his aim is to please the one who enlisted him. An athlete is not crowned unless he competes according to the rules. It is the hard-working farmer who ought to have the first share of the crops. Think over what I say, for the Lord will give you understanding in everything." —2 Timothy 2:3–7

Paul uses three professions—the soldier, the athlete and the farmer to illustrate the perspective and commitment that is needed to multiply spiritually. Note the principles that Paul teaches from these three professions.

The soldier (vv. 3–4)

- A good soldier is single-minded in purpose. He is willing to say no to good things in order to please his ranking officials.

- A good soldier is willing to suffer hardship.

DISCUSS
List some of the things you may consider to be "good things" to which you might have to say no in order to participate in spiritual multiplication.

_____

_____

_____

DISCUSS
What are some difficulties, which someone who is committed to multiplying spiritually might face?

_____

_____

_____

The athlete (v. 5)

- The victorious athlete is disciplined. He knows that hours of rigorous training and discipline lie behind every victory.

- The victorious athlete knows and follows the rules of competition.

DISCUSS

In what ways does one who wishes to participate in mentoring need to be disciplined?

_____

_____

The farmer (v. 6)

- The successful farmer is unafraid of the hard work and patience needed to produce a harvest.

- The farmer enjoys a fruitful harvest. His patience and hard work are rewarded when the harvest is brought in.

DISCUSS

Describe a time when you encountered a relationship that required hard work and patience.

_____

_____

_____

One must spend time studying the Bible and meeting with their discipleship partner. This will establish a great model for your mentoring partner, which will likely carry over into their subsequent mentoring relationships as well.

YOUR LIFE TODAY
Applying the Faith Principle to Spiritual Multiplication

Fill in the following chart based on 2 Timothy 2:3–4. Note your perception of your experience in the left box, and the truth of God's Word in the right box:

YOUR EXPERIENCE	WHAT GOD'S WORD SAYS IN 2 TIMOTHY 2:3–4

Fill in the following chart based on 2 Timothy 2:5. Note your perception of your experience in the left box, and the truth of God's Word in the right box:

YOUR EXPERIENCE	WHAT GOD'S WORD SAYS IN 2 TIMOTHY 2:5

Fill in the following chart based on 2 Timothy 2:6. Note your perception of your experience in the left box, and the truth of God's Word in the right box:

YOUR EXPERIENCE	WHAT GOD'S WORD SAYS IN 2 TIMOTHY 2:6

Review
Faith is choosing to live as though the Bible is true regardless of circumstances, emotions or cultural trends.

Ask
If you choose to live as though 2 Timothy 2:3–6 is true, how would you be living?

Pray
Take a moment to ask God to make these biblical truths a greater reality in your attitudes and actions. Share your thoughts below.

BEFORE YOU FINISH
Your Ministry of Spiritual Multiplication
Take some time to reflect on your ministry of multiplication. Answer the following questions:

Are you able:
- To be committed to spiritual multiplication?
- To be a model for change?
- To look for the potential in others?
- To be committed to live a disciplined life?
- To rely on the Holy Spirit to accomplish all of the above?

What can get in the way of your ministry of spiritual multiplication?

_____

_____

List some of the people you believe are ready to participate in spiritual multiplication:

_____

_____

_____

Ask God to raise up a person with whom you can share this information so that he or she can become a spiritual multiplier, too.

Consider all the material through which you have just worked, and read the following statement. When you completely agree with the statement, sign on the line.

By faith I choose to believe that God is calling me to invest my life in the ministry of spiritual multiplication.

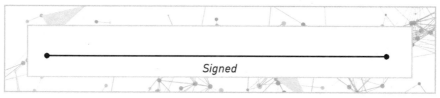

Signed

Made in United States
Troutdale, OR
12/07/2024

25875347R00066